A SCHOOL SURVIVAL GUIDE

HOW TO WRITE TERRIFIC BOOK REPORTS

REVISED EDITION

Elizabeth James and Carol Barkin

Beech Tree
New York

(Previous edition published as
How to Write Your Best Book Report)

For our editor and friend Dorothy Briley,
with thanks and appreciation

In memory of my family, especially Sally, Curt, and
Nancy and Aunt Kay and Uncle Ray, who encouraged my
lifelong love of books and the written word
—EJ

Published by Lothrop, Lee & Shepard Books
an imprint of Morrow Junior Books
a division of William Morrow and Company, Inc.
1350 Avenue of the Americas, New York, NY 10019
www.williammorrow.com

Printed in the United States of America.

The Library of Congress has cataloged the Lothrop, Lee & Shepard Books version of *How to Write Terrific Book Reports* as follows:
James, Elizabeth.
How to write terrific book reports / by Elizabeth James and Carol Barkin.
p. cm.
Includes index.
Summary: Explains how to write an effective book report, covering such aspects as choosing the book, thinking while reading, writing a first draft, and preparing the final draft, and offers tips for oral presentations.
ISBN 0-688-16131-6
1. Report writing—Juvenile literature.   2. Book reviewing—Juvenile literature.   [1. Report writing.   2. Book reviewing.]   I. Barkin, Carol. II. Title.   LB1047.3.J354 1998   372.13028'1—dc21   98-9198   CIP   AC

Revised Beech Tree Edition, 1998
ISBN 0-688-16140-5

10 9 8 7 6 5 4

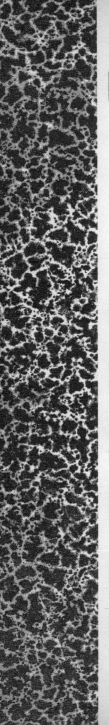

CONTENTS

CHAPTER 1

WHAT IS A BOOK REPORT?

OF COURSE, YOU KNOW WHAT A book report is. It's something your teacher says you have to do!

You may already enjoy writing book reports, and that's great. This book will give you some ideas for making your reports even better.

But there are people who think writing book reports is really boring. Are you one of those people? Do you hate book reports because they are hard to do and because you don't know what to say?

Don't worry—help is on the way! After you read this book, you'll know how to write a book report that's interesting and that's also fun to do.

QUICKIE "BOOK REPORTS"

Have you ever told a friend about a great book you just read? Maybe you said, "It was really exciting," or "It told me just what I wanted to know about volcanoes."

Did your friend ask you what else you liked about the book? You might have said that it was very funny and it made you laugh. Or maybe you said it was easy to understand. Perhaps you especially liked the pictures in the book, or you loved the characters in the story and you wished you knew them in real life.

When you said those things, you were giving your friend a book report. It may have been short, but you were saying what you thought about a book you had read. And that's what a book report is all about.

BOOKS ARE A WAY OF TALKING

When you were little, before you learned to read, your parents probably read books to you. You listened as they read. And those stories from books probably didn't seem much different from the stories your parents made up in their heads to tell you at bedtime. A book is simply a way for an author to write down what he or she wants to tell other people. It's a form of communication. Instead of sitting next to you and telling you in spoken words, the author writes the story on paper so you can read it anytime you want.

A book report is also a form of communication. In a book report, you are telling other people about a book you have read.

WHAT GOOD IS A BOOK REPORT?

You probably think that you would never bother to write a book report unless your teacher assigned it for class. You may be right. But book reports can be very useful.

Thousands of new books are published every year. And that means that there are hundreds of thousands of books available for you to read. That's a lot! Even if you never did anything but read, you would not be able to read every book in the world.

So how can you decide which book to read? How can you tell if it's a book you will enjoy?

This is a difficult problem. But maybe listening to someone else's book report would help you. After all, a book report tells what a book is about and whether one person thinks it's any good.

Suppose there is a book called *Kingdom of the Lions.* And suppose you've been wondering if this is a book you'd like. But you don't even know what kind of book it is. Is it a book of facts about lions in Africa? Is it a made-up story about a character named King Lion and what happens to him? Or could it be an adventure story about a planet where all the "people" are lions?

One way to find out is to ask someone who's read it. Your first question might be, "What kind of book is it?" But there are probably other questions you'd like to ask about the book. Reading a book report can give you the answers.

For a nonfiction book (*nonfiction* means it provides information about real things or real people), a book report can tell you whether the information is accurate. You probably wouldn't want to bother reading a book that doesn't have correct facts. You also might not want to read it if the book report says it is confusing or hard to understand. In that case, you'd want to find a better book on that subject.

What about fiction books? (*Fiction* means stories that are made up.) A book report tells part of the story, so you know what it is about. Also, the report gives one person's opinion of the book. For example, is the story exciting, or too slow and boring? Did the person who read the book care about what happened to the characters?

Of course, even if a classmate says a book is great, you may not like it at all. Or you might love a book that someone else thinks is terrible. But a book report is useful because it lets you know what a book is about and what one person thinks of it.

YOU CAN HELP!

When you write a book report, you're doing an important job for your classmates. Your report is a lot like a book review in a newspaper or magazine. A book review is a short article that tells what a book is about and whether the reviewer thinks it is any good. Many adults read these reviews regularly, because it helps them decide which books they want to read.

In the same way, what you write in your book report may make your classmates want to run right down to the library and check that book out. On the other hand, if your whole class read the same book and hated it, what you say in your book report may let your teacher know why!

What you think about the book you're reporting

on is your opinion. And your opinion is as important as anyone else's. You may think a book is wonderful or horrible or just plain blah. Your book report is the way you communicate your thoughts to other people. After all, they can't read your mind; they can only read the words you write on paper!

CHAPTER 2

CHOOSING A BOOK FOR YOUR REPORT

WITH ALL THE ZILLIONS OF BOOKS in libraries and bookstores, how do you decide which one to read for your report? Sometimes you don't have much choice. Your teacher may give you a short list of books that can be used for your book report. But even so, you'll have to pick one of them to read.

Here are two important things to think about when you're deciding which book to read.

HOW LONG IS IT?

A very long book takes a long time to read. That may seem obvious. And long books can be wonderful and exciting. But if your report is due next week, you may not have time to read that four-hundred-page adventure story.

Think back to the last few books you have read. How long did it take you to finish each of them? This will help you plan how much time you will need to read the book you've chosen. Remember, too, that you'll have to allow extra time for writing the report after you've read the book. So keep length in mind when you pick out the book for your report.

HOW HARD IS IT?

A book that is too difficult for you to read can be a real turnoff. If it's written for older kids or adults, you may find it confusing or frustrating. And it may make you feel stupid if you can't figure out what's going on. So it's a good idea to find a book that you can read fairly easily. But it shouldn't be *too* easy! A book that's meant for really little kids will probably not be very interesting to you, and you won't have much to say about it in your report.

WHAT'S A "GOOD BOOK" FOR YOU?

The most important thing in choosing a book for your book report is to find one that will be fun for you to read. You won't enjoy reading a book that you find boring and uninteresting, and you certainly won't enjoy writing a report about it either. The more fun you have doing your report, the better it is likely to be. And the first step is to find a book you really like.

It's a good idea to keep a list of the books you enjoyed reading. Jot down the title and the author's name and put the list on your bulletin board or in your notebook, or keep a list on your computer. That way, when it's time to choose a book to report on, you can use your list for some clues. Maybe you'll remember that you wanted to read another book by an author on your list. Or maybe you had planned to find out more about a really interesting subject. You can look for a different book on that topic for your report.

But what if you haven't kept a list like this? How can you figure out if you're going to like a book before you read it?

Sometimes it's obvious right away. For instance, if you hate sports, a book called *How to Play Soccer* or *Bobby's Home Run* will be a poor choice. On the other hand, if you love mysteries, a book with the title *The Secret of the Locked Room* may be just what you want.

Sometimes, however, it's not easy to tell from the title what a book is about. And there are lots of times when your mind is a blank and you don't even know what you want! Luckily, there are a number of people you can ask for advice.

WHERE TO GET HELP

Your teacher is the first person to ask for help in choosing a book. After all, he or she probably has some idea of what kinds of books you enjoy and of how well you can read.

But what if none of your teacher's suggestions sounds like what you want? Who else can you ask?

Your friends may have some terrific books to recommend. Maybe your best friend is as crazy about horses as you are, and you can ask her for the titles of her favorite horse stories. Or if you know someone who has read every single one of a twenty-book adventure series, why not ask him which story he liked best?

Your parents also may have some great books to suggest. Does that surprise you? It shouldn't. Your parents may not have read many children's books recently, but you could ask them which books they loved most when they were kids. After all, a book your dad can recall years after he read it must have made a big impression on him. And if the book Dad remembers is still available, there must be a lot of other people who thought it was wonderful, too. So why not give it a try?

A bookstore is one place where you might find that book Dad liked. Another place to find that book—or *any* book—is the library.

CHAPTER 3

A LOOK AT THE LIBRARY

LIBRARIES ARE WONDERFUL PLACES, and they are full of books. In fact, sometimes that's the problem with libraries. Do you ever walk into the library to look for a book and feel that you don't know where to start? Somewhere, hidden on one of those jam-packed shelves, you *know* there's a book you'd love to read. But how do you find it?

Probably you have already learned in school about libraries and how they work. The fiction books are kept separate from the nonfiction. Fiction is arranged on the shelves in alphabetical order by the author's last name. If you're looking for a book by Walter

Farley, you know it will be in the *F*'s—after Fairfield but before Feldman.

So far, so good, right? But what about the nonfiction? All nonfiction books are arranged according to the topics they are about. Books about horses are all together; so are books about airplanes.

Finding the topic you want can be a little tricky, because the topics are not arranged in alphabetical order. Instead, they are arranged according to a system of numbers called the Dewey decimal classification system.

Don't worry—you don't have to learn which number goes with which subject. All you have to do is use the library's catalog; in most libraries, it's on computer. The catalog lists all the books in the library alphabetically according to the title and the author's last name. It also lists nonfiction books, and some fiction books, by subject.

To look up a subject, go to the subject index; ask the librarian for help if you're not sure how to do this. Then type in the name of the subject (such as "guinea pigs" or "lasers") and start the computer search. Soon you'll see a list of books on that subject on the screen. Go to the catalog entry for one of them and jot down its Dewey decimal number.

If you go to the shelf where books with that number are kept, you'll see all the books on that topic.

It's quite easy to do if you know what you're looking for. But often the problem is that you don't have any idea what to look for. You just want a good book to read. So there you are, staring at shelves and shelves of books and wondering what to do.

CALL FOR HELP!

Of course, in a library you wouldn't actually stand there and scream for someone to help you. But do find the librarian and explain your problem. Librarians know a lot about books—that's their job. They can help you figure out where to find the perfect book for your report.

You'll have to give the librarian a few hints to start with, though. He or she can't tell just by looking at you what kind of book you'd enjoy reading. Start out by explaining that you need a book for a book report, and tell the librarian what grade you're in. Most important, try to remember the title of a book you read recently that you liked.

These clues are enough to get things started. Perhaps the librarian will suggest another book by the same author who wrote a book you liked.

Or maybe there's a brand-new book on a subject that interests you. Sometimes there's a book that almost all kids your age seem to enjoy, but you can't remember its title or its author's name. If you describe it, the librarian will probably know which book you mean.

Don't be afraid to talk to the librarian, and don't feel shy because you don't know what you're looking for. Librarians are there to help, and nothing makes them happier than having people like you take books out of the library.

TRY SOMETHING DIFFERENT FOR A CHANGE

It's easy to get into the habit of reading only one kind of book. Maybe you read a mystery that was great, so you just kept reading the same kind of mysteries for months. Or maybe you read a book of jokes and riddles that were really funny, so you kept looking for more books just like it.

There's nothing wrong with that. But after a while, it may get a little boring. Now could be a good time to try something new. Here's an idea that might work for you.

Take a look at the books that are on display in the library. Usually the display has a theme; it could be a holiday, or a topic like "Summer Fun," or a news event like a scientific discovery or a presidential election.

Many kinds of books are likely to be included in a display. For example, if the theme is Halloween, here's what you might see: stories about ghosts and goblins; a nonfiction book about how to make Halloween costumes; another nonfiction book about how trick-or-treating and other Halloween traditions got started; picture books about Halloween; and a book of poems about Halloween night.

Have you ever tried reading poetry? If you haven't, this might be the perfect time to give it a chance. Or maybe you never thought about how Halloween got started. But now that you see the book on display, you think you might enjoy reading it.

Books that are displayed face out, so that you can see their front covers, look inviting and interesting. And it's so much easier to choose one of them than to look through the shelves of tightly packed books. It's too bad that libraries don't have room to show all their books facing out. But if they did, you'd have to walk for miles before you got to the *Z*'s!

Even if you don't choose a book from the display, looking at it tells you how much librarians know about the different kinds of books in their libraries. They have lots of information about books at their fingertips. And since they love books themselves, they're eager to help you find a book that you will love to read.

CHAPTER 4

HOW TO READ A BOOK

OF COURSE YOU KNOW HOW TO read a book—you've probably known how since the first grade! You open it up and start reading on page one, and then you keep on turning pages and reading the words until The End. So what else do you have to know about reading books?

Reading a book for a book report is a little different from reading a book just for your own enjoyment. For one thing, you really do have to read the *whole* book. When you're reading for yourself, you can stop anytime you want to. But for your book report, you can't quit reading partway through. That's one good reason for choosing a book you think you'll enjoy reading.

If you've left your book report until the last minute, you may be tempted to read only a little bit of the book. After all, what's wrong with just taking a look at the beginning and the end of the story?

If you think about it for a minute, it's easy to see why that won't work. First of all, what can you say about a book you haven't read? There's no way you can end up with a book report you'll be proud of if you can only report on the first and last pages. And trying to write a report without knowing what the book says is much harder than reading the book to begin with.

Maybe someone has told you that you can find short summaries of some books on the Internet. Lazy students sometimes decide it's quicker to read a summary than to read a whole book. But although it may take less time, it's not as much fun. You don't get to enjoy the characters and setting, the interesting language, and the fascinating or unusual details that make this book special.

In addition, pretending you've read the book when you haven't is a kind of cheating. You've probably heard that before from your parents and your teachers, and it's still true! The kids who did read the books they reported on will think it's unfair if you didn't read yours. And think of the author who worked hard to write the book; if you formed your opinion without reading it, you didn't give the author and the book a fair chance. Last but not least, you're cheating yourself out of the good grade you could have gotten if you'd read the book in the first place.

THINK AS YOU READ

By now you're curled up in a comfortable chair or sprawled across your bed with your book. It's great when you get so caught up in a story that you can't wait to find out what happens next and you don't even hear your parents calling you to dinner. But it's a good idea to take a break now and then. This gives you time to think about why you like the book so much.

HOW DOES THE BOOK MAKE YOU FEEL?

For example, does the book you're reading make you laugh? If so, what's so funny? Perhaps the characters have a silly way of talking. Or maybe they get themselves into ridiculous situations.

When you figure out just what it is that makes this book funny, you'll be able to explain it in your book report.

Some books can even make you cry. It may sound strange, but reading a story that brings tears to your eyes can be a wonderful experience.

If the book you are reading makes you cry, see whether you can explain why it is so sad. Perhaps something awful happens to one of the characters. A person might get hurt or even die in the story, or an animal might get lost. Reading about these things, even when they happen in a story and not in real life, can make you feel very sad.

But sometimes nothing terrible happens to anyone in the book, and it still brings tears to your eyes. A skillful author can make a character come alive in a way that seems real. It seems as if whatever happens to that person in the story is really happening to you.

What if the main character in the book is embarrassed in front of his class or has a fight with a close friend? A good book can make you feel as if you are that character—when he's unhappy, you may start to cry.

Why would people want to read a book that

makes them cry? Believe it or not, people read these books for the same reason they read books that make them laugh! Sometimes reading about a character who feels the same way you do can help you understand yourself a little better. Maybe you'll see that the mistake you were embarrassed about in school was actually pretty funny. Or perhaps when you read about a character who has a problem sort of like yours, it will make you feel that you're not all alone.

There is another reason why people love to read books, or see movies and plays, that make them feel so strongly. Have you ever heard your parents say that a book was very "touching" or that it "spoke to them"? What they mean is that the story made them have strong feelings or that it said things they wished they could say themselves.

Good writers are able to use words in a way that brings out a reader's own feelings. And when you read a book that makes you laugh and cry, you feel as if you've been part of someone else's life for a little while. No matter whether the story takes place a hundred years ago or right now or even in the future, you move outside yourself while you're reading it. It's very exciting!

DOES THE BOOK TAKE YOU ON AN ADVENTURE?

Some books can transport you to a world that's completely different from your own. Fairy tales and books about magical kingdoms let you follow the amazing stories of characters who could never be real. The author's imagination created this world, and you can use your own imagination to enter it.

Adventure stories can keep you on the edge of your seat, wondering what's going to happen on the next page. These tales may take place in olden times or in the future, or they may seem to be happening right this minute. It's great to feel as if you're sailing with pirates on the high seas or riding with knights in armor. You might find yourself chasing a satellite into a new galaxy, or you could solve a mystery in a town like your own.

When you find a book that's truly exciting, you can hardly stand to put it down. But at the same time, you may want to read slowly so you won't get to the end too soon.

Your book report about this story will probably say that everyone should read the book right away! But your report will be even better if you can explain just *why* the book was so exciting. Did you worry that the main character would get caught by the robbers before the police arrived? Did the author make a huge storm on the ocean sound so dangerous that you felt you might be washed overboard? Saying these things in your report will give other people a good idea of why you liked the book so much.

DOES THE BOOK TELL YOU WHAT YOU WANT TO KNOW?

Nonfiction books can be exciting in a different way from fiction books. Since nonfiction tells you about things that are true, nonfiction books don't have made-up characters or imaginary stories. But real life is often very interesting! Wouldn't you like to read a good book about dinosaurs or about how magicians do their tricks? Or maybe you'd enjoy a biography (a book about a person's life) of a famous movie star or of the first person to reach the North Pole.

While you're reading, remember to stop now and then to think about why you like the book. Does it explain things clearly so you can understand them? If it is a biography, does it make you feel that you really know that person?

Like fiction, nonfiction books can take you to

places you've never been before. A book on astronomy can send you into outer space, while one on whales will show you the amazing world under the sea. Books about history let you do some time traveling. For instance, a biography of Abraham Lincoln can tell you what it was like to live in America more than one hundred and fifty years ago.

Some nonfiction books may make you a little sad. When you read about the unhappy times in a person's life, you'll probably feel sorry for him or her. And a book on animals that are in danger of dying out may even make you cry. It's awful to realize how many kinds of animals may soon become extinct. But a book like this could give you ideas on how to help change things.

There are also lots of nonfiction books that are amusing. A book about dogs may have funny true stories about the author's own pets. Another book might make you laugh at all the troubles Alexander Graham Bell had while he was inventing the telephone. Some authors are able to explain things in a way that is both interesting and funny. Humor can help you remember the facts better after you've finished reading the book.

Thinking about what you read while you're reading it makes writing your book report easier. It gives you some specific things to say in your report, and you'll be able to remember what you did and did not like about the book.

CHAPTER 5

GETTING ORGANIZED

NOW THAT YOU'VE READ THE BOOK, it's time to get started on the book report. But wait—don't start writing yet! Take a few minutes first to think about what you want to say and how your ideas can be organized. This will make writing your report faster and easier.

Your teacher has probably given you some rules for writing your book report. Perhaps you got a list of questions with space to write the answers. Maybe you copied down the directions for writing your book report from the blackboard. Or you may have taken notes when the teacher discussed book reports with the class. If you didn't do those things, check with a friend so you'll know exactly what your assignment is.

Now is the time to make sure you have all the information you need to write your book report. Here are some things you should know:

1. How long must your book report be?
2. When is it due?
3. What questions should your report answer?

WHAT SHOULD YOUR BOOK REPORT SAY?

Most book reports for school contain the same kinds of information. First, of course, you have to include the title of the book you read and the name of the author. Then you'll need to tell what kind of book it is, a little about the subject or the story, and what you thought about the book. For a short book report, that may be all you have room to say.

If you are writing a longer report, there are other things you can include. Maybe your teacher wants you to describe one of the characters or explain a new fact you learned. But the main questions are pretty much the same for any book report.

If your teacher wants you to do your book

report in a certain way, of course that's the way you'll do it! But if you're not sure how to do it or how to get started, the next few pages will help you. And you may find that the questions your teacher gave you are almost the same as the ones in this book.

HOW TO BEGIN

If you're writing your book report by hand, you need three sheets of paper. They will be the first draft of your report—that means you will copy it over neatly after it's finished. So you don't have to worry too much about neatness now!

Write one of these three questions at the top of each page:

1. What is the book about?
2. What main idea did the author want to tell the reader?
3. Did you like the book or dislike it? Why?

If you're writing your first draft on a computer, type in these three questions.

These questions will be the main topics of your report. You will write one or two paragraphs to answer each of them.

Thinking about the answers to these questions is the most important part of doing a book report. When you've figured out what you want to say, you'll be ready to start writing.

CHAPTER 6

WRITING THE FIRST DRAFT

UNLESS YOU'VE DONE A LOT OF book reports before, you may think it's a dumb idea to write a first draft. It might seem like a waste of time and energy to do the work twice. But almost everyone finds that it's by far the easiest way to write anything!

When you write the first draft of your report, you have a chance to concentrate on what you want to say. It's like a practice test—it doesn't count, and you don't hand it in to your teacher.

This means that you can cross things out if you change your mind. You can make sure what you've written is the right length. And you can keep on changing it until you're certain you have used just the right words. Of course, if you're using a computer to write your first draft, making changes will be even easier.

Ready to go? The first thing to do is put the title of the book and the author's name above the first question. Then start right in.

QUESTION 1: WHAT IS THE BOOK ABOUT?

Is your book fiction or nonfiction? Remember that fiction is a made-up story about imaginary characters, while nonfiction books tell about real people or about things that happen in the real world.

NONFICTION BOOKS

A nonfiction book has a subject or topic. But most books can't tell you everything there is to know about that subject. So your book report should explain what part of the main topic the book covers.

Suppose your report is on a book called *How to Keep a Secret: Writing and Talking in Code,* by Elizabeth James and Carol Barkin (the authors of this book!). *How to Keep a Secret* is a nonfiction book about codes and ciphers. But what about them exactly? The book explains the way many different codes and ciphers work. It tells you how to use them yourself.

The first paragraph of your report might look like this:

> This nonfiction book is about codes and ciphers. It tells how to use a lot of different codes. After you read it, you'll know how to write notes to people in code.

Notice that you say right at the beginning that the book is nonfiction.

In the second paragraph, you can say a little more about what is in the book. Pick out something you especially enjoyed and tell why you liked that part. For example, you might describe one of the codes and explain how it works.

What other information does the book give? If you have room to say more, you could mention that it tells some of the history of codes and that it gives ideas for forming a secret club with your friends.

If your report includes all these things, it will give a good picture of what this book is about.

FICTION BOOKS

What about book reports on fiction? When you tell what the book is about, the problem is to keep it short! It's tempting to tell the whole story from beginning to end. Of course, you can't do that. Your book report would be much too long. Also, it would spoil the book for other people if you told too much.

See if you can explain what the book is about in just a few sentences. If you were doing a book report on *4B Goes Wild,* by Jamie Gilson, you might say:

> This is a funny story about Hobie Hanson and his friend Nick. They are in fourth grade, and they go on a school trip for three days to Camp Trotter. A lot of funny and scary things happen to them there.

By using the word "story" in your first sentence, you let other people know that this book is fiction. "Story" and "novel" are only used to describe fiction.

For your second paragraph, pick out one of the things that happens in the book and tell it in another couple of sentences. This will give people an idea of what to expect in this book. But don't explain *everything* about what happens. For instance, you might tell about how Hobie and Nick sneak out to the cemetery at midnight. But you shouldn't reveal what happens when they meet the skunk. You don't want to spoil the surprise for other readers!

It's very hard to explain what a book is about in just a few sentences. It takes a lot of thought. But that's how you end up with a good book report instead of just a retelling of the book in different words.

When you are ready to describe your book, write your description on the first sheet of paper or type it under the first question on the computer.

QUESTION 2: WHAT MAIN IDEA DID THE AUTHOR WANT TO TELL THE READER?

The main idea of a book is not the same as the topic or the story. It is a "bigger" idea that sums up the whole book. One way to think about it is to ask yourself, Why did the author want to write this particular book? What meaning did the author want readers to get from the book?

NONFICTION BOOKS

In nonfiction books, the author's reason for writing the book is to help readers learn more about a certain subject. But the main idea of the book is probably more than that.

For example, a book on dog training tells you how to go about teaching your dog to obey you. That is what the book is about. But the main idea might be something like this: "Training your dog properly makes both you and your dog happier together." That's what the author wants you to understand after reading his book.

In *How to Keep a Secret: Writing and Talking in Code,* you can tell from reading the book that the authors really enjoyed playing around with codes. You already know that the book is about codes and ciphers and how to use them. But you may decide that the main idea of the book is something like this:

> Codes are a lot of fun to learn about. You can have a good time using codes with your friends. It's like playing a secret game.

FICTION BOOKS

Sometimes it's harder to figure out why authors of fiction have written their books. But an author chooses to write a story because it has a special meaning for him or her. Often the meaning of a fiction book has something to do with important things like love or courage or honesty.

It's only after you finish reading a story that you can think about what it means. Instead of asking yourself what happened to the main character, try to figure out what the character learned. Did the character change or look at things differently by the end of the book? Thinking about this gives you a clue to the story's meaning.

After reading *4B Goes Wild,* you might say something like this about the main idea:

> Hobie is afraid to spend two nights away from home, but he doesn't want anyone to find out he feels this way. By the end of the book, Hobie has learned that camp was okay and he can have fun being away from home at camp.

Of course, someone else who reports on the same book could come up with a different main idea.

That doesn't mean that either of you is wrong. One of the wonderful things about books is that people don't always look at them in the same way.

When you decide what you think the main idea of your book is, write it down on the second sheet of paper or type it under the second question on the computer.

QUESTION 3: DID YOU LIKE THE BOOK OR DISLIKE IT? WHY?

It's easy to answer the first part of this question! But figuring out exactly what it was that made you love or hate a book is a little harder.

Think back to how you felt as you read the book. This will give you some ideas. When you have figured out a few of your reasons for liking or not liking the book, you can write them on the third sheet of paper or type them in under this question.

NONFICTION BOOKS

What are some of the things you might have enjoyed about a nonfiction book? Maybe you learned something new and fascinating, like how far a bullfrog can jump. Perhaps the book explained eclipses so clearly that you finally understood them for the first time. The book may have had beautiful photographs of animals in the desert. Or did you like the way the author made little jokes now and then, like when he said his dog teamed up with his cat to catch mice?

All of these are excellent reasons why you might like a nonfiction book. In your report, it's a good idea to write down a specific example or two to show what you mean, instead of just saying "It was funny" or "I learned a lot." This makes your report more interesting to read, and it also helps other people find out if it's the kind of book *they* would enjoy.

Let's suppose that you read *How to Keep a Secret* for your report and liked it a lot. Here's what you might say under this third question:

> This was a terrific book because it explained the codes in a funny way. I liked the parts where the authors pretended the kids really acted like spies. And the coded messages in the book were neat. When you decoded them, they told a silly story.

FICTION BOOKS

What are some things you might like about a fiction book? Maybe the main character reminded you of your best friend or told great jokes all the way through the book. Perhaps the book was full of exciting adventures that you wish would happen to you. You'd love to find a bag of gold hidden in an attic! Or what happened in the story may have seemed so real that you felt you were right there on the covered wagon crossing the plains.

If *4B Goes Wild* was the book you were reporting on, you could say something like this:

> I liked this book because almost everything that happened in it was funny, but it was still like real life. I thought it was neat when Hobie figured out that the story about his parents getting a divorce was like the Telephone game they played at camp. The best and funniest part of the book is about a cat, but I don't want to spoil it for you by telling what it is. I think everyone should read this book!

WHAT IF YOU DIDN'T LIKE THE BOOK?

Even if you didn't like the book you read, you can use it for your book report. A book review that says a certain book is boring or repetitious helps people decide whether they want to read it, and your book report can do the same thing. If you really didn't think the book was good, you should say so. There isn't any reason to pretend you liked it or to feel bad about your opinion. But you still need to give your reasons.

A nonfiction book might have been hard to understand because the author explained things so poorly. Perhaps it contained information that is no longer correct, like saying there are forty-eight states in the United States. Or maybe the author kept repeating the same thing over and over, and that made the book boring.

In a fiction book, you might have thought the characters did such dumb stuff that no one could believe in them. Maybe the characters were nice enough, but nothing much happened in the story and you didn't care how it ended. Or did you think the characters were such nasty people that you didn't like reading about them?

Your explanations of why you liked or disliked the book you read should be clear enough for other people to understand. Your feelings about the book are part of what makes your book report interesting and useful.

PUTTING YOUR REPORT TOGETHER

When you have written what you want to say under the three questions for your report, you have to put the three sections together. The questions themselves will not be part of your report. They are only guidelines to help you keep your thoughts organized.

If you wrote by hand on three pieces of paper, stick them together with tape. Attach the first, second, and third sections to make one long sheet of paper. You can either cut off the questions at the top of each section or tape the papers so that the questions are covered up. But leave some blank space between the sections so you have room to make changes if you need to.

Of course, if you wrote your answers to the questions on the computer, you can just delete the questions and any extra space you left between the sections. Then print out the report. This makes it easier to work on.

Now you are ready to read through your whole book report and see how it sounds.

CHAPTER 7

DOING THE FINAL DRAFT

THE FIRST VERSION OF YOUR BOOK report, or of any piece of writing, is called a first draft. As you read through your first draft, you're sure to find things that should be changed or fixed up before you make a final copy to hand in. Even famous authors who have written lots of books don't expect the first draft to be perfect.

You have already spent time and effort working on your book report. Now is your chance to make it as good as it can possibly be.

COMMON PROBLEMS AND HOW TO FIX THEM

There are certain problems that many

people have when they are writing book reports. Here are some hints on what to do about them.

THE REPORT IS TOO LONG

Often this is because you've told too much of what the book is about. Check the first section of your report and see if you can shorten it. One way to do this is to try using just the first and last sentences of this section. Maybe you don't need all the explanation in between. Or cross out every other sentence in the first section and see if what's left makes sense. Remember, you shouldn't be telling everything that is in the book.

THE REPORT IS TOO SHORT

Maybe this is because you didn't take enough time to write down your thoughts. Did you give complete answers to all the questions? After you look over your report, see if you can add a description of an event in the story or an interesting fact you learned. This will make your report a little longer and also more fun to read.

YOU DIDN'T SAY WHAT YOU MEANT

Sometimes when you reread what you've written, you realize that it just doesn't sound right. Your report sounds as if you loved a book you really hated, or as if you thought the book was dumb when you actually felt it was funny and clever.

The best way to fix this is to read your report very slowly. After each sentence, stop and ask yourself if just that one sentence says what you meant to say. If it doesn't, cross it out and write a better one. Then go on to the next. When you're finished, your report should sound just the way you want it to.

WHAT ARE YOU TALKING ABOUT?

Remember, the person who reads your book report probably hasn't read the book. So you have to make sure that the person can tell who or what you mean in each sentence. If you keep writing "he," will other people know you mean the boy and not the old man? Using the character's name or a phrase like "the little boy" helps keep things clear.

PARAGRAPHS ARE TOO LONG OR TOO SHORT

Your book report should have at least three paragraphs—one paragraph for each question you answered. And you may have had enough to say to make five or six paragraphs altogether.

If you have a paragraph that goes on for most of a page, it's too long! Read it over to yourself. You'll probably find a place where one paragraph should end and a new one should begin.

On the other hand, a paragraph that has only one short sentence in it is too short. Perhaps you have a little more to say about this topic. Or maybe this sentence really belongs in the paragraph before it or the one after it.

SENTENCES ARE TOO LONG OR TOO SHORT

Sentences that run on and on make a book report almost impossible to read. If you see that your sentences go on for several lines before coming to a period, break them up. Try to make two or more shorter sentences out of each giant one. Then see if your report is easier to read.

The opposite problem is having a whole bunch of short, choppy sentences. Some of these very short sentences can be put together into longer ones by using "and" or "because" between them.

If you have both short and long sentences in your book report, it will be much easier to read.

DID YOU REPEAT YOURSELF?

It's pretty boring to read a report in which all the

sentences sound almost the same. Do several of your sentences start out with "And then they said . . ." and "And then they went . . ."? If so, you can change some of them by using words like "later" or "afterward."

Another problem that happens in book reports is too many sentences that start with "I." Does your whole last section say "I think" and "I like" at the beginning of every sentence? Maybe you could change a sentence like "I liked the part on the boat best" so that it says "The part on the boat seemed the best to me" or "The part on the boat was great." Changing things so your sentences don't all sound the same helps make your book report fun to read.

READING YOUR BOOK REPORT ALOUD

Ask one of your parents or a friend to read your report aloud while you listen. This is a good way to check what you've got. Sometimes you can hear a problem that you didn't notice when you read the report to yourself.

Perhaps you have left out a word here and there. Someone else trying to read your report will catch this right away. Or you might hear the same word popping up over and over again. Listening to your own report gives you a chance to find and fix things like this.

If there's no one around to read your report to you, read it out loud to yourself. You'll hear any problems in your writing just as well this way. And besides, it's good practice for giving an oral report to the class.

WRITING THE FINAL DRAFT

When you're happy with all the changes you've made in the first draft, it's time to write your final draft. Get out the instructions your teacher gave you and make sure you know how the book report should look. Here are some things to check:

1. Where do you write your name and the date?
2. If you're writing by hand, should you use pen or pencil?
3. Do you write on every other line of the paper? For reports typed on a computer, do you double-space?
4. Do you write on one side of the paper only?

Probably the title of the book you read will be

the title of your report. Your teacher may have told you how to do this. If not, a good way is to write the title on one line and the author's name on the next line, like this:

4B Goes Wild
by Jamie Gilson

Now you can copy your book report neatly with all the changes you made, or you can type in the changes and then print the report in its final form. Remember that the three questions you used to organize your report should not be included. They were just to help you think about what to say where.

THE FINISHING TOUCHES

Before you hand in your book report, take time to check it over very carefully. Make sure all the words are spelled correctly and that punctuation is where it should be. It's easy to leave out a period or put in the wrong letter when you're concentrating on your writing, and now is the time to catch these errors.

Even if you use a spelling checker on the computer, it's important to look for mistakes yourself.

You might have typed "there" when you meant "their." If it's spelled correctly, the computer doesn't know it's the wrong word. Grammar checkers also don't catch some kinds of mistakes, so you need to read your report carefully to make sure it's okay.

When you're sure your book report is just the way you want it, you can feel good about it as you hand it in. You'll know you've done your best work.

SAMPLE BOOK REPORTS

On the next pages are the final drafts of the book reports on *How to Keep a Secret* and *4B Goes Wild*. If you look carefully, you can see that the writers made small changes to improve their first drafts.

These final drafts are ready to turn in. The first paragraph of each report explains what the book is about, and the second paragraph goes on to describe one specific part of the book. The third paragraph tells the book's main idea. And the fourth paragraph gives the report writer's opinion about the book.

Even if you read one of these books, your book report on it wouldn't sound exactly like the ones in this book. Your report should give your own ideas and opinions. But these samples show you how a book report can be put together using the three main questions discussed in this book:

1. What is the book about?
2. What main idea did the author want to tell the reader?
3. Did you like the book or dislike it? Why?

BOOK REPORT
How to Keep a Secret: Writing and Talking in Code
by Elizabeth James and Carol Barkin

This nonfiction book is about codes and ciphers. It tells how to use a lot of different codes. After you read it, you'll know how to write notes to people in code.

One code that is easy to do is the backward alphabet cipher. You just write the regular alphabet and then put a backward alphabet above it, so *A = Z*. Then you write your message using the backward alphabet instead of the regular one. In this code my name is Nb Mznv!

Codes are a lot of fun to learn about. You can have a good time using codes with your friends. It's like playing a secret game.

This is a terrific book because it explains the codes in a funny way. I liked the parts where the authors pretend the kids really act like spies. And the coded messages in the book made me laugh. When you decode them, they tell a silly story.

BOOK REPORT
4B Goes Wild
by Jamie Gilson

This is a story about Hobie Hanson and his friend Nick. They are in fourth grade, and they go on a school trip for three days to Camp Trotter. A lot of funny and scary things happen to them there.

One thing that happens at camp is funny and sad at the same time. Hobie and his group are learning about bird banding and no one wants to hold the bird. Finally Hobie holds it. He knows the bird is scared and wants to go home. He understands how the bird feels. The funny part is that all the kids are scared to hold a tiny bird. But the sad part is that Hobie feels so homesick.

Hobie is afraid to spend two nights away from home, but he doesn't want anyone to know he feels this way. By the end of the book Hobie has learned that he can have fun being away at camp.

I liked this book because almost everything that happened in it was funny, but it was still a lot like real life. It was neat when Hobie figured out that the story about his parents getting a divorce was like the Telephone game they played at camp. The best part of the book is about a cat, but I don't want to spoil it for you by telling what it is. I think lots of people would enjoy this book.

CHAPTER 8

EASY EXTRAS

DOES YOUR TEACHER GIVE EXTRA credit for doing extra work? Even if that doesn't happen in your class, it never hurts to do a little more than you are asked to do. Doing extra work might surprise you. It may not be difficult, and it could be fun!

What kinds of extra things could you do for your book report? Here are some ideas.

FIND OUT ABOUT THE AUTHOR

A book doesn't just magically appear on the shelves all by itself. First, someone has to write it! Learning something about the author of the book you read might give you some clues about why he or she wrote that book. You might discover that the author of a book about a horse lives on a ranch in Wyoming and has loved horses all her life. Or maybe you'll find out that the author of an adventure story about Africa has never traveled more than fifty miles from his hometown in Ohio!

Where can you get this information? The first place to look is in the back of the book you read. If it is a hardcover book with a paper jacket on it, there is often a paragraph or two about the author on the back flap (the part of the jacket that folds inside the back cover). A paperback book may have information about the author printed on the back cover itself. And in some books you can find this information on a page at the end of the book.

While you're looking through the book, see if there is a list of other books by the same author. If you liked the one you read, this is a good chance to find out the titles of more books you will probably enjoy. Sometimes a list appears on the back flap of a hardcover book jacket and on the back cover of a paperback. Or you may find a list on one of the first pages of the book, before the book itself starts.

TRY THE LIBRARY

If you can't find any facts about the author in the book you read, you may have better luck at the library. Remember that some books are printed in both hardcover and paperback. You could look for a hardcover copy of a book you read in paperback, and perhaps it will give you some author information.

Another possibility is to check other books by the same author. Different information about his or her life may appear in different books.

Ask the librarian if your library has any reference books about authors. These books don't list every author, but there's always a chance that the author of your book will be included. Often there is a lot more information in a reference book than there is on the back flap of a jacket. So you may want to look up your author even if you've already found out something about him or her.

If the book you read has pictures, you may want to find out more about the illustrator. Information about the illustrator is usually in the same place in the book where you find facts about the author. And there are also reference books about illustrators in many libraries.

LOOK ONLINE

Another place to look for facts about an author or illustrator is the Internet. Some authors and illustrators have Web pages that provide lots of information about them and their books. You may learn all sorts of things. One author may describe the farm he grew up on in Minnesota. Another might say that the chemistry experiments she did in high school inspired her to write about science. Still another could post a photo of her three-legged cat—the star of her funny stories.

GET IN TOUCH WITH THE AUTHOR

Most authors enjoy hearing from the people who read their books. Naturally, everyone likes praise, and any author is happy to get mail or e-mail that says "I loved your book!"

But there are other things you can write to an author about. Do you have specific questions about the book you read? For instance, you may wonder whether the author really knew a person like one of the characters.

Some authors answer all their mail from readers and others don't. If you write a letter, make it easy for an author to reply to you. Print your name and address clearly on your letter and on the envelope. And it's polite to enclose a self-addressed, stamped envelope for the author to use when he or she writes back to you.

Remember that you are writing to someone you don't know. Like anyone else, authors don't usually like to give out information about their personal lives. A home address is considered personal information, so you will have to send your letter in care of the publisher. Mail it to the author at the publisher's address, and someone there will forward it to the author for you. You can write to an illustrator in the same way. Look at page 63 of this book to learn how to find a publisher's address.

If you know an author's e-mail address, you can send your questions or comments about a book that way. But even using e-mail doesn't guarantee that you'll get an answer.

If you don't get an answer, don't be discouraged. Maybe the next author you write to will send you a great letter you can share with all your friends.

WRITE TO THE PUBLISHER

What is a publisher? A publisher or publishing house is a company that turns an author's typed pages into a printed book and sells it. It's usually easy to find out the name and address of a book's publisher. Turn to the copyright page of the book you read for your report. This page is often near the front of the book, and it usually has a lot of small print on it. The publisher's name, and usually the address, are included along with other information. For example, near the beginning of this book you will find the words "Copyright © 1986, 1998 by Elizabeth James and Carol Barkin."

Here is what the whole copyright notice of this book looks like:

Do you see that the publisher's name is Lothrop, Lee & Shepard Books? Then comes the address you can write to.

If the publisher's address isn't in the copyright notice, ask the librarian to help you look it up in a reference book.

Another way to find a publisher's address is to look on the Internet. Many large publishing houses have Web sites where you can find their addresses (regular and e-mail), along with lots of information about their books. Notice that the copyright page of this book contains the Web site address of the publisher: www.williammorrow.com

ASK FOR INFORMATION ABOUT THE AUTHOR

Many publishers can send you short biographies of some of the authors and illustrators whose books they publish. These biographies are usually one page long, with a photo of the author or illustrator at the top.

Since the book you read was probably written specifically for kids, you should send your letter to the Children's Books Marketing Department. Be sure to put your full name and address on your letter so the person who gets it will know where to write back to you. Remember to be polite; the people who work for publishers are usually very busy and may take quite awhile to answer your letter.

Also, if you are asking for something to be sent to you, it's only fair for you to pay for the postage. Enclose an empty unsealed envelope addressed to you and put a stamp on it.

Of course, if your book report is due soon, there may not be time to write to the publisher and get an answer. It's also possible that the publisher has nothing to send you about this author or illustrator.

Even if there's not much time, you may decide to write to the publisher. Maybe in a month or two you will get an answer, and you can use it for a report on another book by the same author.

ASK FOR FREE STUFF!

It's true—sometimes you can get something for nothing, or for just the price of a postage stamp. Publishers often have bookmarks, posters, newsletters, and catalogs that they use to publicize their books. Write to the Children's Book Marketing Department and ask for any free material they have about the book you are reporting on.

The publisher will not have free items about every book, and you may not get an answer to your letter right away. However, if you are in luck and the publisher sends you enough bookmarks for your whole class or a great poster you can put on the wall, it will be worth the wait.

EVERYBODY MAKES MISTAKES SOMETIMES

This probably won't help you with your book report, but here's another reason to write to a publisher. As you read your book, you may have found that it had some mistakes in it. Publishers try very hard to make sure there are no mistakes in their books. But of course, nobody's perfect! Sometimes you see a word that is spelled wrong. Or sometimes a word is printed twice when it shouldn't be, like this: He sat down in the the chair.

If you find a mistake, the publisher will be glad to know about it so it can be corrected the next time the book is printed. Your letter should tell the title of the book the mistake is in, the author's name, the page number where you found the mistake, and, of course, what the mistake is!

Address this letter to the Managing Editor of Children's Books. Be sure to include your name and address on your letter. If the managing editor is polite, you'll get a note thanking you for being so observant.

CHAPTER 9

GIVING AN ORAL REPORT

HAS YOUR TEACHER ASKED YOU TO give an oral book report? You may hate the whole idea, but an oral (spoken) report can be a lot of fun. The secret is to know what you're doing when you stand up in front of the class.

You may want to read your written book report out loud. On the other hand, you might prefer to talk about the book instead of reading your paper.

Reading your report to the class has some advantages. The words you are going to say are written on your paper, so you won't get tangled up in sentences that don't have endings. Also, if it makes you nervous to talk in front of the class, you'll probably feel most comfortable reading your report.

However, if you choose to talk about your book instead of reading your report, you'll be able to look at the people who are listening to you. Your eyes won't be focused on the paper in your hands the whole time. If you look at your audience, people will feel that you're talking directly to them.

Of course, you'll be giving the same information in your talk that you put in your written book report. The difference is that you'll be making up the sentences as you speak instead of reading them.

It's a good idea to make notes on the main things you plan to tell the class. This will keep you from forgetting the things you wanted to say. Many speakers use index cards for their notes. On each card, you can write a few words about one main point you want to make. Print your notes in big letters so you can read them easily with just a quick glance.

Whichever way you decide to give your report, be sure to practice it a few times at home. Remember to:

1. Stand up nice and straight.
2. Speak clearly so each word can be understood.
3. Talk slowly—don't rush.
4. Try not to fidget!

Maybe your parents will be your practice audience. They'll appreciate knowing how hard you've worked on your book report! Or perhaps there is a tape recorder you can use for a rehearsal. You may be surprised at the way your voice sounds on tape. Nobody's voice sounds exactly the same on tape as it does in real life. But at least you can find out whether you are talking too fast or stumbling over your words.

Another good way to practice giving your report is to stand in front of a full-length mirror. This makes it seem as though you're talking in front of another person.

No matter how you practice, you'll want to know if you're keeping to the time limit your teacher has set. Use a timer or check the clock to measure the length of your oral report. This lets you know whether you need to make your report a little longer or shorter.

You may think it's a waste of time to practice

giving your book report. But it really isn't. The experience of saying your report out loud a couple of times will make you feel much better about doing it in class. And the more relaxed you feel, the better job you'll do when it's your turn to give your oral report.

PROPS AND COSTUMES

If you have something to show to the class during your oral report, it can make your report more interesting. In addition, having a prop or two to hold up or pass around gives you something to do besides just standing there. That's always a help if you get nervous when you speak in front of an audience.

One good prop is the book you read for your report. If it has illustrations you really like, put slips of paper in the book to mark those spots. Then it will be easy to open the book to the right page and hold it up so everyone can see. And of course, you can show everyone the cover of the book at the beginning and the end of your report.

Sometimes it's easy to think of a prop that will help you tell what your book is about. For a science book, perhaps you can do a simple experiment that you learned from the book. If you read a book about magic tricks, it would be great to practice one and perform it during your report. You could even wear a magician's costume.

Books that take place in the past or the future can give you some ideas for costumes. You could give your report in a pirate outfit just like the one the main character in your book wore. But you don't have to wear a complete costume. A patch over one eye and a bandanna around your head would be enough. Use your imagination! An old hat or scarf or some weird jewelry might give you a look that goes with your book.

For a book report on *How to Keep a Secret: Writing and Talking in Code,* it's hard to think of a costume. But there are lots of props you could use. Why not make one of the secret coding devices in an extra-large size? Then you can show it to the class and explain how it works. Or if you are reporting on *4B Goes Wild,* you could bring along a hairy rubber hand or a flashlight.

Extras like props and costumes are fun, but they are certainly not necessary. Lots of books are great to read even though they don't seem to have any possibilities for props or costumes. Don't worry if you can't think of a single thing to use. After all, what's important is what you have to say about the book.

However you decide to give your oral report, take time to plan and practice in advance. With all the work you've put into it, you can feel sure that this will be a terrific book report.

CHAPTER 10

OTHER WAYS TO "REPORT" ON BOOKS

BESIDES WRITTEN AND ORAL BOOK reports, there are many other ways to tell people about a book you've read. If your teacher says it's okay, why not try something different instead of—or in addition to—your regular book report?

WRITE A DIARY OR JOURNAL ENTRY

It's fun to imagine yourself as one of the characters in the book you read. A fiction book gives you lots of characters to choose from. But some nonfiction books, especially biographies, are full of interesting people, too. Once you've picked out a character, you can think about what that character might have written in a diary or a journal.

To do this, you have to "think" yourself inside the character. The book gives you clues about what kind of person the character is and what he or she thinks and believes. You could write a diary about the events in the book, giving that character's point of view about what happened. If you choose a person who is not the main character in the book, his or her thoughts about the events may turn out to be very different from those of the main character.

You can also make up new situations that aren't in the book. Then you'll have to think yourself into the character's mind so you can figure out how he or she would act in the situations you make up. A good way to get started is to imagine what might have happened after the end of the story.

Remember, however, that you're not inventing the character. He or she should stay the same way as in the book. If a boy in the book was afraid to swim in the ocean, he should be afraid in the diary entries you write. Or if a girl loves dogs in the book, she shouldn't hate them in your journal entries.

As you write the diary or journal, you can refer to other characters and events from the book. Perhaps you'll have your character make a diary entry about the cousin who visited in the book. Maybe you'll write about cleaning up after the big storm that happened at the end of the book.

Writing a character's diary or journal can make the book seem even more real to you. It's fun to think about the people and places in the story. This kind of writing can help you get to know them even better.

SEND SOME MAIL

Letters and e-mail are other ways of writing from a character's point of view. You could compose a letter from one character to another, or from a character to you. Then you could write answers to these letters, from you or from the other character.

You can do the same with e-mail, or you can work with a partner. Two characters from the book might e-mail each other. This can be kind of funny, especially if your book takes place in colonial America, when there were no computers—in fact, there was no electricity to run them!

To get started, think of some news your character might want to tell someone in a letter. Maybe you'll have your character write a thank-you note for a gift. What about a letter to a pen pal in another country? Then your letter could describe the character's family and the place where he or she lives.

Be sure to start your letters with "Dear [Whoever]" and end them with "Sincerely yours" or whatever sounds right for your character. For e-mail, modern characters might be quite casual, just like you and your friends. But a character from the eighteenth century would probably write in a more formal-sounding way, even on a computer.

Letters and e-mail can be great ways to tell about a nonfiction book. For a book about Alexander Graham Bell, why not write a letter from Mr. Bell to his friend, explaining why he invented the telephone?

MAKE UP A SKIT

Do you like to perform in skits and plays? Here's your chance! With one or two partners, try writing a skit based on the book you read. Think back to a part of the book that was especially exciting or interesting. Then figure out how many characters will be needed for your skit.

Some of the dialogue in your skit will probably be what the characters say in the book. But you might have to write extra dialogue for the parts that were described with no conversation. Try to have the characters speak the way they do in the book. If one of them uses a phrase like "Oh, wow!" all the time, be sure to include it in the new dialogue you write.

Another possibility is to have a narrator for your skit. This is a good way to tell the audience things they need to know in order to understand what's happening in the skit.

When you present your skit, remember to speak clearly so you can be heard. And when it's over, be sure to take a bow!

REPORT THE NEWS

Writing a newspaper article is a great way to "report" on a nonfiction book. Your article will present the information from the book as if it were news. Include interesting details to make the article fun to read. And be sure to explain why the information is important. For instance, maybe the information in a book about earthquakes can help people build houses in a safer way.

Remember, a news article is different from a book review. Newspaper articles shouldn't include opinions, so you won't write about why you liked or disliked the book.

There's another way to write a newspaper article about the book you read. Pick out one part of the book and write only about that part. For instance, if you read a book about earthquakes, you could write a news article about one big earthquake as if it had just happened. Or you could write about the invention of the telephone, pretending that the news media just found out about it today. Of course, you'll still include lots of other information from the book, as "background" for your news article.

All of the different ways of reporting about a book tell people what that book is like. It's fun to think about which kind of report will work best for a particular book. And who knows—maybe you'll enjoy doing book reports so much that you'll decide later on to get a job as a book reviewer! Even if you don't, the book reports you do now help other people decide which books they can't wait to start reading.

If you'd like to read the books used for reports in this book, here's the information you need:

How to Keep a Secret: Writing and Talking in Code
by Elizabeth James and Carol Barkin
Hardcover from Lothrop, Lee & Shepard Books:
ISBN 0-688-16277-0
Paperback from Beech Tree:
ISBN 0-688-16278-9

4B Goes Wild
by Jamie Gilson
Hardcover from Lothrop, Lee & Shepard Books:
ISBN 0-688-02236-7
Paperback from Pocket Books:
ISBN 0-671-68063-3

INDEX